STRAIGHT FORWARD

English Series

Sentences

by S. Harold Collins

Book cover design by Kathy Kifer

Published by:
Garlic Press
605 Powers St.
Eugene, OR 97402

ISBN 0-931993-41-5
Order Number GP-041

www.garlicpress.com

Dear Parents, Teachers, and Students:

The Straight Forward English Series has been designed for parents, teachers and students. The Series is composed of books designed to measure, teach, review, and master specific English skills. The focus of this book is sentences.

What makes this Series different?

- Various textbook series have been compared. The Straight Forward English Seriespresents the skills crucial to mastery of sentences as reflected by major English textbooks.

- Sentence skills are concisely explained, practiced, and tested.

- Mastery can be measured by comparing the Beginning Assessment Test with the Final Assessment Test.

- This series has more content and no distracting or unrelated pictures or words. The skills are straightforward.

How to use this book.

- Give the Beginning Assessment Test to gain a starting measure of a student's sentence skills.

- Progress through each topic. Work the exercises. Exercise work can be done in the book or on a separate sheet of paper. Set a standard to move from one topic to the next. If the standard is not met, go back and refocus on that skill.

- Give the Final Assessment Test to gain an ending measure of a student's sentence skills. Compare the skill levels before and after this Final Assessment Test.

Table of Contents

A. Complete Subject-Complete Predicate. Draw a vertical line between the complete subject and the complete predicate.

1. Her trip lasted two months.
2. The last chapter ended quickly.
3. Every person laughed.
4. Some children came later.
5. Bright flowers decorated the yard.

B. Simple Subject-Simple Predicate. Underline the simple subject once and the simple predicate twice in Section A.

C. Subject-Verb Agreement. Choose the correct word in parentheses.

1. I (want, wants) to attend the movie.
2. (I, She) am hungry.
3. The hat and coat (was, were) left behind.
4. (Winter, Winters) is cold in this country.
5. Squirrels (chase, chases) our cat.

D. Sentence Structure. Identify each sentence as one of the following: a simple sentence, a compound sentence, a sentence fragment, or a run-on sentence.

1. My aunt is a fine teacher she teaches seventh grade.
2. We went to see the polar bears, but they were resting.
3. The cat chased the mouse.
4. Had lost the direction home.
5. Call me, and I will come.

E. Combining Sentences. Combine each pair of sentences to make one simple sentence.

1. Elaine wants to come. Jacob wants to come.
2. My uncle buys furniture. My uncle sells furniture.

Sentences

Kinds of Sentences

A **sentence** is a group of words that express a complete thought. A sentence begins with a capital letter and ends with a period (.), or a question mark (?), or an exclamation point (!).

There are four types of sentences.   Example

•Declarative	
A declarative sentence tells something. It ends with a period.	The temperature is warm.
•Interrogative	
An interrogative sentence asks something. It ends with a question mark.	Is it warm?
•Imperative	
An imperative sentence gives an order or makes a request. It ends with a period.	Please find out how warm it is. OR Find out how warm it is.
•Exclamatory	
An exclamatory sentence shows strong feeling. It ends with an exclamation mark.	It is hot !

Sentences, Exercise 1. Identify each sentence as declarative, interrogative, imperative, or exclamatory.

1. What a beautiful day it is!
2. Set the table.
3. Will you set the table?
4. The jacket was a birthday present.
5. Please get those boxes.
6. The weather was terrible yesterday.

7. What a fine new car you have!
8. How did you find the answer?
9. Do what I said, right now!
10. The project should be finished tomorrow.

Sentences, Exercise 2. Identify each sentence as either declarative, interrogative, imperative, or exclamatory.

1. I don't believe my eyes!
2. Look up the address in the phone book.
3. Can you help this person next?
4. We will be home in four hours traveling at this speed.
5. Compare the two blue houses.
6. My father is flying home today.
7. Is there time to call a friend?
8. How beautiful these flowers are!
9. Another serving will be enough for me.
10. Read the story for yourself.
11. Please tell us exactly what happened.
12. Sometimes people make mistakes.
13. What a strange sight!
14. Have you seen the decorations downtown?
15. I can only guess.

Sentences, Exercise 3. Write two original examples of each sentence type: declarative, interrogative, imperative, and exclamatory.

Subject and Predicate
Complete Subject – Complete Predicate

All sentences have two parts, the subject and the predicate. The **subject** tells who or what the sentence is about. The **predicate** tells something about the subject.

•Complete Subject and Predicate

All words that tell who or what the sentence is about make up the **complete subject**.

All words that tell something about the subject make up the **complete predicate**.

Complete subject	Complete predicate
The cat	ran behind the sled.
Peru	is in South America.
One person after another	disappeared into the cave.
The small garden	was full of roses and tulips.
The tall man	laughed.

The complete subject or complete predicate can be one word or more than one word.

Complete Subject-Predicate, Exercise 1. Draw a vertical line between the complete subject and the complete predicate.

1. My father was born here.
2. My brother and sister were not born here.
3. Our family moved to Oregon last year.
4. We enjoy the state.
5. It rains often.
6. Not everyone likes the rain.
7. The McKenzie River flows through our small town.
8. Many interesting people live here.
9. We went on a picnic last weekend.
10. My mother and father invited the next-door neighbors.

11. Everyone roasted hot dogs.
12. I ate two hot dogs.
13. My mother, father, brother, and sister swam.
14. The picnic ended after dark.
15. Joan and Paul slept late the next day.

Complete Subject-Predicate, Exercise 2. Are the underlined words the complete subject or the complete predicate?

1. They <u>came by plane.</u>
2. <u>Red, white, and blue banners</u> decorated the house.
3. Rita, Elena, and Juan <u>left.</u>
4. <u>The light</u> hung from the ceiling.
5. A sad clown <u>waved to the crowd.</u>
6. <u>I</u> ran, skipped, and jumped all the way.
7. <u>A silver moon</u> glowed brightly in the sky.
8. Denver <u>is the capital of Colorado.</u>
9. <u>Canada and the United States</u> share a common border.
10. Our group <u>hiked six miles before lunch.</u>

Complete Subject-Predicate, Exercise 3. Underline each complete subject once. Underline each complete predicate twice.

1. Our cat sleeps on Emily's bed.
2. Her name is Molly.
3. Molly and our family live in a small house.
4. Emily, Elena, or Dad feeds Molly.
5. Molly yowls if she is not fed on time.
6. Our neighbor's cat looks similar to Molly.
7. Most younger cats chase string, snakes, and mice.
8. Some older cats are wiser.
9. The next-door neighbor watches Molly when we are gone.
10. Cat owners have responsibilities.

Subject and Predicate

Simple Subject – Simple Predicate

The **simple subject** is the main word that tells who or what the sentence is about. A simple subject is a noun or pronoun. A simple subject is the most important word in the complete subject.

The **windows** on the porch   are dirty.
The **children** in our neighborhood   play after school.
They   play together well.

In these three examples, the complete subjects are underlined and the simple subjects are in **bold** print. **Windows** and **children** are simple subjects. **They** is both a simple subject and a complete subject.

Sometimes the simple subject may have several words that name a person or a place.

Raymond Jackson   lives across the street.

Simple Subject-Predicate, Exercise 1. The complete subject is underlined. What is the simple subject?

1. Our vacation begins on Friday!
2. I can hardly wait.
3. Mrs. Norton is traveling to Iowa.
4. The leaves on the ground were brown, tan, and red.
5. The fastest runner was John Martin.
6. Two young raccoons watched.
7. She asked the operator many questions.
8. My friend called late last night.
9. Many other people followed us to the store.
10. His arm was broken in two places.
11. The houses closest to the park burned.
12. The beautiful flowers decorated the yard.
13. They want to travel east.
14. The capital of South Dakota is Pierre.
15. Some children came late.

Simple Subject-Predicate, Exercise 2.   Underline the simple subject.

1. We built a house next door.
2. All short people stood in front.
3. The San Juan Islands are in Washington state.
4. I ran to the window first.
5. The red bows were tied last.
6. The calm lake shone in the moonlight.
7. Many lives were in danger.
8. The lives of many people were in danger.
9. Yosemite National Park is in California.
10. One was taken.
11. The book was found much later.
12. The last chapter ended quickly.
13. Each of us has a special job.
14. One person complained to the owner.
15. Her trip lasted six months.

Subjects in Imperative and Interrogative Sentences.

What are the simple subjects in these sentences?

Imperative: Answer the phone for me.

Interrogative: Can you answer the phone for me?

The subject of an imperative sentence is not always stated. Usually the subject is understood to be *you*.

(You) Answer the phone for me.

The subject of an interrogative sentence can be found by dropping the question mark and rearranging the word order to make a sentence:

Can you answer the phone for me? = You can answer the phone for me.

How far shall I go? = I shall go how far.

Simple Subject-Predicate, Exercise 3. What is the simple subject of each sentence?

1. Did Maria find her books?
2. Ask someone else.
3. Shall I call you?
4. Sit in the last row.
5. Follow me to your seat.
6. Should I ask for directions?
7. What are my chances of losing it?
8. Are you finished with the book?
9. Hold this for me.
10. Test the engine first.
11. Clean the front windows.
12. Did you clean the front windows?
13. Hold your pencil in your right hand.
14. What do I do?
15. How will you get there?

The **simple predicate** is the most important word in the complete predicate. The simple predicate is always a verb. The simple predicate is the main word that tells about the subject.

The children **ran** to the playground.
Recess **is** their favorite time.

The simple predicate may be more than one word. The simple predicate may be a main verb and a helping verb.

The children **have played** at the playground.
They **will be playing** there today.
They **were playing** there a few minutes ago.

Simple Subject-Predicate, Exercise 4. The complete predicate is underlined. What is the simple predicate?

1. Our vacation begins next Friday!
2. Should I ask for directions?
3. Mrs. Norton is traveling to Iowa.
4. The leaves on the ground were brown, tan, and red.

5. (You) <u>Ask someone else.</u>
6. Two young raccoons <u>watched.</u>
7. He <u>talks on the phone two hours a day.</u>
8. The children <u>played together well.</u>
9. <u>Did</u> you <u>clean the front windows?</u>
10. My arm <u>is broken in two places.</u>
11. They <u>have been gone all day.</u>
12. The beautiful flowers <u>decorated the yard.</u>
13. (You) <u>Hold this for me.</u>
14. The capital of South Dakota <u>is Pierre.</u>
15. Some children <u>came later.</u>

Simple Subject-Predicate, Exercise 5. Underline the simple predicate.

1. We built a house next door.
2. All short people stood in front.
3. The San Juan Islands are in Washington State.
4. I ran to the window first.
5. The red bows were tied last.
6. The calm lake shone in the moonlight.
7. Many lives were in danger.
8. Do you know where to go?
9. Yosemite National Park is in California.
10. One has been taken.
11. It was found much later.
12. The last chapter ended quickly.
13. Each of us has a special job.
14. One person complained to the owner.
15. (You) Clean the porch!

Simple Subject-Predicate, Exercise 6. Review. Underline the simple subject once. Underline the simple predicate twice.

1. Some people have gone early.
2. Can you go with us?
3. We watched.
4. Its shape makes it one of the fastest cars.
5. The group of boys left on the bus.
6. Help me put this on the shelf.
7. These insects can surprise you.
8. The two crew members walked aboard ship.
9. The clown with the red nose wore a big hat.

10. Children sat quietly.
11. The very last car was painted blue.
12. Every person laughed.
13. I remembered everything later.
14. How many boxes did you buy?
15. John Mills rode to school with me.
16. Her eyes sparkled with delight.
17. He was running too fast.
18. Our family will have Thanksgiving together.
19. Please bring your own meal.
20. Mickey Mouse had his own television show.

Subject and Predicate

Compound Subject - Compound Predicate

When a sentence has two or more subjects joined by *and* or *or*, the subject is called a **compound subject**.

Nick, Miles, *and* Elena went to school.
The women *and* men worked hard.
Jane *or* her father left.
The Greeks *and* Romans told stories.

When a sentence has two or more predicates joined by *and* or *or*, the predicate is called a **compound predicate**.

She <u>left</u> school *and* <u>returned</u> home.
The syrup <u>dripped</u>, <u>splashed</u>, *and* <u>oozed</u>.
The noise <u>surprises</u> *or* <u>frightens</u> everyone.
She <u>learned</u> to act *and* <u>became</u> a star.
They <u>played</u> instruments *or* <u>sang</u> songs.

Compound Subject-Predicate, Exercise 1.   Underline the compound subjects.

1. Mom and Dad went dancing.
2. Are carrots or beets cheaper?
3. Dogs, cats, birds, and fish are at the pet store.
4. Elena or her mother bought the present.
5. Red, yellow, and blue are primary colors.
6. He and I went to the party.
7. Mary, Joan, or their mother will be there.
8. The doctor and her patient talked.
9. The letters, books, and newspapers filled the mailbox.
10. Six or seven cars and trucks drove quickly past.
11. My uncle or your aunt has the answer.
12. Jane, Fred, and I rode the bus.

13. Violins and violas are string instruments.
14. You or I must answer their questions.
15. Pens, pencils, and erasers will be needed.

Compound Subject-Predicate, Exercise 2. Underline the compound predicates (verbs).

1. We stood and waited.
2. Elena and Emily dance and sing.
3. (You) Clean or cut the meat.
4. Our school band meets and practices on Tuesday.
5. She wrote books and became famous.
6. Albert walks home or rides the bus.
7. The visitors watched a movie or went home.
8. He coughed and sneezed.
9. They raked leaves, piled wood, or burned branches.
10. Some farmers raise and sell wheat.
11. (You) Please return to the boat and get your pole.
12. They drove to the store and bought food.
13. Michael and I ran home, grabbed our bags, and returned here.
14. The adults wrote letters and sent them by mail.
15. I ate dinner, read the newspaper, and went to bed.
16. We went to the car and returned with the groceries.
17. The shoes were too small and had worn soles.
18. He gave us instructions and left.
19. The family sat, ate their lunch, and played games.
20. They grow thick fur and have bushy tails.

Compound Subject-Predicate, Exercise 3. Underline any compound subjects once and any compound predicates twice.

1. Alice and Maria laughed and cried.
2. She loved art and became a painter.
3. The cat or the bird left first.
4. Many people ride the bus or drive their car.
5. Our mother and father went to the store and bought food.
6. Trains or cars pass every few hours.
7. The program began at 7:00 P.M. and lasted 3 hours.
8. Sleet, snow, or rain is predicted for today.
9. Tom poured a glass of milk and drank it.
10. I will call or write.
11. Trees and bushes burned.
12. The hot water boiled wildly.
13. Deer, elk, and moose fill the woods.
14. Smoke and steam rose from the earth.
15. The dog walked to the fence, barked at the cat, and lay down.

Subject and Predicate

Subject – Verb Agreement

The subject of a sentence must agree with its verb. If the subject is singular, use a singular form of the verb. If the subject is plural, use a plural form of the verb.

Present Tense Verbs	
<u>Singular Subject</u> Add *s* or *es* to verb.	The bird sits on the wire. The bird watches everything. The bird flies away.
<u>Plural Subject</u> Do not add *s* or *es* to the verb.	The birds sit on the wire. The birds watch everything. The birds fly away.
<u>Pronouns</u> I or You– use the plural form of the verb.	I like to watch birds. You go with the others.

Subject-Verb Agreement, Exercise 1. Select the verb in parentheses which correctly completes each sentence.

1. He (drive , drives) across the mountains.
2. I (want , wants) to attend the show.
3. The sun (rise , rises) at 6:00 A.M.
4. The apple trees (blossom , blossoms) soon.
5. My parents (live , lives) in Canada.
6. Squirrels (chase , chases) our cat.
7. She (call , calls) me often.
8. My sister Jane (want , wants) to be a writer.
9. My father (encourage , encourages) her to write.
10. Everybody (enjoy , enjoys) a good laugh.
11. He (run , runs) five miles a day.
12. We (know , knows) where to eat.
13. You (fix , fixes) it yourself.
14. He (fix , fixes) it himself.
15. It (fall , falls) slowly.

Subject-verb agreement sometimes becomes confusing when **irregular verbs** are used. Forms of the verb *to be* are especially confusing.

Singular Present/Past		Plural Present/Past	
I am	I was	we are	we were
you are	you were	you are	you were
he is	he was	they are	they were
she is	she was		
it is	it was		

Remember: Singular subject, use a singular verb. Compound subject, use a plural verb.

Subject-Verb Agreement, Exercise 2. Select the word or words that will correctly complete each sentence.

1. (John and Susan , He) were going to the beach.
2. I (am , are) the person to talk to.
3. My brothers and sisters (was , were) here before sunset.
4. He and I (am , are) traveling together.
5. The flowers and lawn (is , are) covered with leaves.
6. (Winter , Winters) is cold in this country.
7. The (sandwiches and shakes , hamburger) were ready.
8. (I , She) am hungry.
9. (My parents , My sister) are in Canada.
10. You and I (is , are) responsible for finishing the project.

Compound Subject and *And*

When the parts of a compound subject are joined by **and**, use a plural verb.

Max, John, **and** I <u>talk</u> frequently.
Mother **and** Jane <u>are</u> here for lunch.
Our friends **and** neighbors <u>were</u> excited.

Subject-Verb Agreement, Exercise 3. Which verb correctly completes the sentence?

1. You and he (is , are) responsible for finishing the project.
2. Cities and towns (has , have) bus transportation.
3. Many books and letters (was , were) found in the drawer.

4. Wind, rain, and snow (make , makes) driving difficult.
5. Juan, Marta, and I (am , are) friends.
6. Cars and buses (causes , cause) traffic problems.
7. The faucet, hose, and sprinkler (works , work) well.
8. A hat and coat (was , were) left behind.
9. The window and door (closes , close) easily.
10. The van and truck (is , are) in the driveway.
11. The man and woman (was , were) walking together.
12. A burger and fries (cost , costs) only two dollars.
13. Bill and Martha (has , have) the entire set.
14. You and I (am , are) going to the show.
15. An orange, apple, and pear (is , are) mixed in the salad.

Subject-Verb Agreement, Exercise 4. Think of a compound subject to complete these sentences.

1.	live down the street.
2.	are wild animals.
3.	were complete.
4.	are months.
5.	are species of fish.
6.	have ordered parts.
7.	sleep standing up.
8.	follow directions.
9.	were correct.
10.	cost money.

Sentence Structure

Sentence Fragments

A sentence is a group of words expressing a complete thought. A group of words that does not express a complete thought is a **sentence fragment**.

Sentence fragments are missing a subject, or a predicate, or both a subject and a predicate.

- **Missing Subject** - Who or what are these sentence fragments about?

  Can run fast
  Bought a newspaper and milk

- **Missing a Predicate** - What did the subject do?

  My friend Susan
  Many tall buildings

- **Missing Subject and Predicate**

  From the house
  In the yard
  Which was full
  Through the door and around the corner

Sentence Fragments, Exercise 1. Are these complete sentences or sentence fragments?

1. The house was red.
2. Red, blue, and green.
3. The dog and kittens.
4. Ran through the woods and into the house.
5. In the morning before breakfast.
6. The phone rang late at night.
7. Yelled the frightened man.
8. All along the road.
9. Outside and far away.
10. Opened the door and left.

11. Call me!
12. First, second, or third.
13. Ran and sat down.
14. Near our house and theirs.
15. Can you come?

Sentence Fragments, Exercise 2. Tell whether each group of words is: (a) a complete sentence; (b) needs a subject; (c) needs a predicate; or, (d) needs a subject and predicate.

1. An elephant in the zoo.
2. Played the violin.
3. An elephant in the zoo played the violin.
4. In a minute or two.
5. Built their house.
6. From six miles away.
7. Will you come with me?
8. My sister, cousins, and uncle.
9. With the paper in his hand.
10. Six wild deer.

Sentence Fragments, Exercise 3. Make complete sentences from these sentence fragments as the parentheses direct.

1. With your help   (add subject and predicate)
2. Left the front door open   (add subject)
3. Tall trees and bushes   (add predicate)
4. Books, newspapers, and letters   (add subject and predicate)
5. In a corner   (add subject and predicate)
6. The loud noise   (add predicate)
7. Had lost the direction home   (add subject)
8. Was surprised by the lightning   (add subject)
9. Suddenly my friend   (add predicate)
10. The hinge from the gate   (add predicate)
11. Enjoyed the party   (add subject)
12. On Friday afternoon   (add subject and predicate)
13. Had been sleeping   (add subject)
14. Back and forth   (add subject and predicate)
15. When the bell rang   (add subject and predicate)

Sentence Structure

Simple Sentences

The sentences you have studied so far have been simple sentences. A **simple sentence** expresses one complete thought. A simple sentence has a complete subject and predicate.

Four Types of Simple Sentences
•**Simple Subject-Simple Predicate**   The cat chased the mice.   •**Compound Subject-Simple Predicate**   The cat and dog chased the mice.   •**Simple Subject-Compound Predicate**   The cat chased and caught the mice.   •**Compound Subject-Compound Predicate**   The cat and dog chased and caught the mice.

Simple Sentences, Exercise 1. This exercise is mostly a review. All sentences are simple sentences. Label each sentence as one of the following: (a) simple subject-simple predicate; (b) compound subject-simple predicate; (c) simple subject-compound predicate; or, (d) compound subject-compound predicate.

1. The fire, police, and rescue people were ready and waiting.
2. They returned home and washed.
3. Patrick and I walked to the store.
4. (You) Come with me to the store.
5. My brother and sister are at school.
6. My parents walked or ran home today.
7. The house was painted red and decorated with signs.
8. The cat or the dog tracked mud into the house.
9. I caught two fish after six hours of fishing.
10. The wind was warm.
11. Nancy and Susan cooked hot dogs and roasted marshmallows.
12. The door or window is open.
13. I cleaned my coat and hung it up.
14. Robert and Ann read books or watched television.
15. We left.

Sentence Structure

Compound Sentences

A **compound sentence** combines two or more simple sentences which have related ideas. The simple sentences are joined by connecting words (conjunctions) like *and*, *or*, and *but* . A comma is used before the connecting word.

I went to the show, **and** John went to the museum.
I could go to the show, **or** I could go to the museum.
John couldn't go to the show, **but** he could go to the museum.

Use *and* if the second simple sentence adds more information to the first. Use *or* if the two simple sentences give a choice. Use *but* if the simple sentences give a contrast or a different point of view.

Compound sentences join two or more simple sentences with a connecting word and a comma:

I went to the show.
    , **and**
+ John went to the museum.

I went to the show, and John went to the museum.

The drive to Portland is long.
    , **but**
+ The scenery is beautiful.

The drive to Portland is long, but the scenery is beautiful.

It will snow tonight.
    , **or**
+ It will rain.

It will snow tonight, or it will rain.

Mother wants us to buy dessert for dinner tonight.
   , but
+ Johnnie likes banana cream pie.
   , and
I like chocolate cake.

Mother wants us to buy dessert for dinner tonight, **but** Johnnie likes banana cream pie, **and** I like chocolate cake.

Sonny goes fishing on Sundays.
   , and
Pamela goes to aerobics on Tuesdays.
   , but
+ They make time to have lunch together on Fridays.

Sonny goes fishing on Sundays, **and** Pamela goes to aerobics on Tuesdays, **but** they make time to have lunch together on Fridays.

Compound Sentences, Exercise 1.   Are these sentences simple sentences or compound sentences?

1. The people worked hard and slept soundly.
2. I can draw, and you can paint.
3. Many birds flew to the fountain and bathed.
4. Do you like blueberries, or do you like strawberries?
5. I heard a funny story, but I have forgotten it.
6. She picked apples or shelled walnuts.
7. The eagle soared above the seagulls and terns.
8. I don't always understand, but I trust your judgment.
9. Bricks, lumber, and cement were delivered here and stored in the shed.
10. The newspaper was wet, and some pages were torn.

Compound Sentences, Exercise 2. Combine these simple sentences to make compound sentences.

1. You can drive north.   (or)
   You can drive where you want.
2. The reporter called yesterday.   (but)
   She didn't come until today.
3. You can take me to the theater. (and)
   I will walk home.
4. Can you find out now?   (or)
   Can you ask me later?

5. We went to see the polar bears. (but)
   They were resting elsewhere.
6. Some animals are endangered. (and)
   They should be protected.
7. You must pay the full price. (or)
   You can't buy the clothes.
8. Most people are not disturbed. (but)
   Some are easily disturbed.
9. She used to play soccer. (but)
   Now she plays racketball.
10. Call me. (and)
    I will come.

Compound Sentences, Exercise 3. Underline the two simple sentences that make up any compound sentence. Circle the connecting word that is used to join the two simple sentences.

1. It is raining now, but it snowed last night.
2. You can bring your boots or shoes.
3. I can finish in no time, or I can take a long, long time.
4. We went fishing, and James caught two fish.
5. She doesn't know why, but she can find out.
6. Bring everything, and we will know the answer.
7. People ran home or walked quickly by.
8. Cups and saucers are there, and forks and knives are here.
9. Our house is closed, but your school is not.
10. The computer stopped and never started again.

Compound Sentences, Exercise 4. In each of the following short paragraphs, use **or, and,** or **but** to combine at least two simple sentences. Answers may vary.

1.   Our family is planning a vacation. My parents want to go to the ocean. My brother and I want to go to the mountains.

2.   My brother likes to hike. I like to collect rocks. Our parents aren't interested in hiking or rock collecting.

3.   Our parents like to swim. They like to sun bathe. We are not the slightest bit interested in swimming or sun bathing.

4.   Perhaps our family can go to the beach. Perhaps our family can go to the mountains. Our parents can go their way. We can go ours.

Sentence Structure

Run-On Sentences

A **run-on sentence** is two or more sentences that run together.

Run-on sentences run two or more thoughts together. It is difficult to tell where one thought ends and the next thought begins.

Here are examples of run-on sentences:

My aunt is a fine teacher she teaches seventh grade.
Her students learn everyone loves her.
She has taught science she has won a national award.

Correcting Run-on Sentences

•**Making Separate Sentences:** Separate each thought into a sentence of its own.

My aunt is a fine teacher. She teaches seventh grade.

•**Making a Compound Sentence Using a Conjunction:** Combine simple sentences using a comma and a conjunction (and, or, but).

Her students learn, and everyone loves her.

•**Combine Subject and Predicates from Separate Sentences:**

She has taught science and (she has) won national awards.

Run-on Sentences, Exercise 1. Correct these run-on sentences in two ways: (a) separate each into two sentences; then, (b) write them together as a compound sentence. Do not begin a sentence with a conjunction.

  1. My brother drove us to the beach we went swimming.
      Separate:
      Compound:
  2. You think that is the answer I don't think so.
  3. Regular plates can break plastic plates break less often.
  4. Some people finish quickly and they have nothing to do.
  5. I never forget you never remember.

Run-on Sentences, Exercise 2. Rewrite these sentences so that they are not run-on sentences.

1. You should call or you should write.
2. I wish you were here someone asked for you.
3. I don't like diet soda I sometimes drink it at parties.
4. Some people have answers some people have questions.
5. I went home I called you.

When the word **and** is over-used in a sentence, it creates a run-on sentence. You lose your breath before the sentence ends. For example:

It rained very hard all day and night and our pond overflowed and covered the road and no one could drive into town.

This sentence would sound better if it was broken into smaller thoughts:

It rained very hard all day and night. Our pond overflowed and covered the road. No one could drive into town.

We might even want to break the compound sentence (*Our pond overflowed and covered the road.*) into two simple sentences:

Our pond overflowed. It covered the road.

Run-on Sentences, Exercise 3. Separate these run-on sentences into smaller thoughts.

1. He sat at the table and looked out the window and watched the wind blow and the sky turned dark and rain fell.
2. They walked down the path and into the woods and Pam climbed a tree and John picked wildflowers.
3. We often buy stale bread and feed the ducks and they swim from all over to get our bread and we enjoy feeding them.
4. Find the telephone book and look up the number and I will call and order a pizza.
5. The bus stopped and the door opened and many people hurried to their jobs and most people arrived on time.

Combining Sentences

•Simple Sentences make Compound Sentences

You have already learned how to combine simple sentences with related ideas to make a compound sentence:

> I went to the show.
>   , and
> + <u>John went to the museum.</u>

> I went to the show, and John went to the museum.

•Compound Subjects

Sentences with compound subjects are really two or more similar sentences combined into one. The similar subjects are joined by *and* or *or*.

> Roberto and Beth will paint the house.
>   Roberto will paint the house.
>   Beth will paint the house.

> Paint, brushes, and a roller will be needed.
>   Paint will be needed.
>   Brushes will be needed.
>   A roller will be needed.

When you combine subjects into one sentence, remember that the verb must agree with the subjects.

> <u>Elaine</u> **wants** to come.
>   <u>Elaine</u> and <u>Jacob</u> **want** to come.
> <u>Jacob</u> **wants** to come.

> <u>Earth</u> **has** a moon.
>
> <u>Saturn</u> **has** moons.   <u>Earth</u>, <u>Saturn</u>, and <u>Pluto</u> **have** moons.
>
> <u>Pluto</u> **has** moons.

Sentence Combining, Exercise 1. Combine these simple sentences into one sentence.

1. No cats are allowed. (or)
   No dogs are allowed.

2. Cars stopped traffic.
   Buses stopped traffic. (and)
   Trucks stopped traffic.

3. You checked the water supply. (and)
   I checked the water supply.

4. Did Bill answer the phone? (or)
   Did Ann answer the phone?

5. A coat will keep you warm.
   A hat will keep you warm. (and)
   Gloves will keep you warm.

6. Martin travels to Albany each day. (and)
   Marian travels to Albany each day.

7. Asia has tall mountains. (and)
   Africa has tall mountains.

8. Neptune is larger than Mercury.
   Saturn is larger than Mercury. (and)
   Jupiter is larger than Mercury.

9. John was home for the summer. (and)
   I was home for the summer.

10. Paint is needed.
    A brush is needed. (and)
    A roller is needed.

Sentence Combining, Exercise 2. These sentences have compound subjects. Write a simple sentence for each subject.

1. Jane and I hid behind the bench.
2. Sun, wind, and rain weathered the boulders.
3. Oranges, apples, and bananas are on sale this week.

4. Those explorers and inventors lived years ago.
5. Nancy and Maria finished the job earlier than expected.
6. Cars or trucks made deliveries in the early morning.
7. Hard work, talent, and luck paid off.
8. He or she will be there at five o'clock.
9. The driver and her assistant arrived late.
10. Eric or his brother will attend the meeting.
11. Elena and Carol write newspaper stories.
12. You and I were in Hawaii last year.
13. Fog and rain slow traffic on the freeway.
14. Nepal and Chile have high mountains.
15. The dog and cat are asleep.

•Compound Predicates

Sentences with compound predicates are really two or more sentences with the same subject combined into one sentence. The predicates are joined by *and* or *or*.

My uncle buys and sells furniture.
     My uncle buys furniture.
     My uncle sells furniture.

The squirrel found, cracked, and ate the walnut.
     The squirrel found the walnut.
     The squirrel cracked the walnut.
     The squirrel ate the walnut.

Sentence Combining, Exercise 3. Combine these simple sentences to make compound predicates.

1. Julia entered the tournament. (and)
   Julia won the tournament.
2. You must go. (or)
   You must stay.
3. We helped with painting. (or)
   We went shopping.
4. My father writes books.
   My father prints books. (and)
   My father sells books.
5. She sat by the phone. (and)
   She waited.

Combining Sentences, Exercise 4. These simple sentences have compound predicates. Write a complete sentence for each predicate.

1. Emily writes or telephones her grandmother every week.
2. The doctor examined, treated, and released the injured worker.
3. I made ornaments and delivered them.
4. The birds built nests or gathered worms.
5. He completed his work and left.
6. My sister reads books and writes letters on Sunday.
7. The crowd pointed and cheered.
8. They cut, stacked, and burned the logs.
9. The sight surprised and frightened them.
10. (You) Ask her or hang up.

Combining Sentences, Exercise 5. Combine the sentences in parentheses.

(Emily walked to the store. Elena walked to the store) (They bought a newspaper on the way. They mailed letters on the way.) (They returned home. They put the groceries away.) (Cans were put in the cupboard. Bottles were put in the cupboard.) (Meat was put in the refrigerator. Vegetables were put in the refrigerator.)

(Emily cut bread. Emily made sandwiches.) (Elena poured milk. Elena set the table.) (They ate lunch. They went outside.)

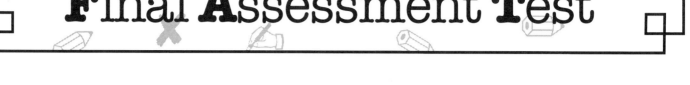

Final Assessment Test

A. Subject-Predicate. Draw a vertical line between the complete subject and the complete predicate. Underline the simple subject once. Underline the simple predicate twice.

1. Can you call my parents?
2. Elena, Marie, and Philip attended the concert.
3. The loud noise startled or frightened everyone.
4. She cut, stacked, and covered the wood.
5. The two young children watched.
6. Calm down.
7. Alice and John laughed and cried.

B. Subject-Verb Agreement. Choose the correct word in parentheses or fill in the blank.

1. You and he (is, are) to meet here later.
2. A hot dog and chips (cost, costs) two dollars.
3. They (was, were) thirsty.
4. _____ have ordered their dinner.
5. _____ are waiting for us.
6. _____ follows me home everyday.

C. Sentence Structures. Identify each sentence as one of the following: a simple sentence, a compound sentence, a sentence fragment, or a run-on sentence.

1. The bus stopped and everybody got off and they crossed the street.
2. Be sure to call me.
3. Hundreds of people.
4. My brother hid, and I counted to twenty.
5. My brother and I counted and hid.

D. Sentence Combining. Combine the three sentences in Part 1 to make a simple sentence. Combine the two sentences in Part 2 to make a compound sentence.

1. The chicken is cooked. The corn is cooked. The beans are cooked.
2. You bought socks. I bought socks.

Answers

Beginning Assessment Test, page 1.

A. Complete Subject-Complete Predicate. Draw a vertical line between the complete subject and the complete predicate.
   1. Her <u>trip</u> | <u>lasted</u> two months.
   2. The last <u>chapter</u> | <u>ended</u> quickly.
   3. Every <u>person</u> | <u>laughed</u>.
   4. Some <u>children</u> | <u>came</u> later.
   5. Bright <u>flowers</u> | <u>decorated</u> the yard.

B. Simple Subject-Simple Predicate. Underline the simple subject once and the simple predicate twice in Section A.

C. Subject-Verb Agreement. Choose the correct word in parentheses.
   1. I (**want**, wants) to attend the movie.
   2. (**I**, She) am hungry.
   3. The hat and coat (was, **were**) left behind.
   4. (**Winter**, Winters) is cold in this country.
   5. Squirrels (**chase**, chases) our cat.

D. Sentence Structure. Identify each sentence asone of the following: a simple sentence, a compound sentence, a sentence fragment, or a run-on sentence.
   1. My aunt is a fine teacher she teachers seventh grade. **Run-on**
   2. We went to see the polar bears, but they were resting. **Compound**
   3. The cat chased the mouse. **Simple**
   4. Had lost the direction home. **Fragment**
   5. Call me, and I will come. **Compound**

E. Combining Sentences. Combine each pair of sentences to make one simple sentence.
   1. **Elaine and Jacob want to come.**
   2. **My uncle buys and sells furniture.**

Sentences, Exercise 1, page 2.

1. Exclamatory	6. Declarative
2. Imperative	7. Exclamatory
3. Interrogative	8. Interrogative
4. Declarative	9. Exclamatory/Imperative
5. Imperative	10. Declarative

Sentences, Exercise 2, page 3.

1. Exclamatory	8. Exclamatory
2. Imperative	9. Declarative
3. Interrogative	10. Imperative
4. Declarative	11. Imperative
5. Imperative	12. Declarative
6. Declarative	13. Exclamatory
7. Interrogative	14. Interrogative
	15. Declarative

Sentences, Exercise 3, page 3.
Answers will vary.

Complete Subject- Predicate, Exercise 1, page 4.

1. father	was born	8. people	live
2. sister	were	9. We	went
3. family	moved	10. father	invited
4. We	enjoy	11. Everyone	roasted
5. It	rains	12. I	ate
6. everyone	likes	13. sister	swam
7. River	flows	14. picnic	ended
	15. Paul	slept

Complete Subject-Predicate, Exercise 2, page 5.

1. Compl. predicate	6. Compl. subject
2. Compl. subject	7. Compl. subject
3. Compl. predicate	8. Compl. predicate
4. Compl. subject	9. Compl. subject
5. Compl predicate	10. Compl. predicate

Complete Subject-Predicate, Exercise 3, page 5.
1. Our cat   sleeps on Emily's bed.
2. Her name   is Molly.
3. Molly and our family   live in a small house.
4. Emily, Elena, or Dad   feeds Molly.
5. Molly   yowls if she is not fed on time.
6. Our neighbor's cat   looks similar to Molly.
7. Most younger cats   chase string, snakes, and mice.
8. Some older cats   are wiser.
9. The next door neighbor   watches Molly when we are gone.
10. Cat owners   have responsibilities.

Simple Subject-Predicate, Exercise 1, page 6.
1. vacation
2. I
3. Mrs. Norton
4. leaves
5. runner
6. raccoons
7. She
8. friend
9. people
10. arm
11. houses
12. flowers
13. They
14. capital
15. children

Simple Subject-Predicate, Exercise 2, page 7.
1. We
2. people
3. San Juan Islands
4. I
5. bows
6. lake
7. lives
8. lives
9. Yosemite National Park
10. One
11. book
12. chapter
13. Each
14. person
15. trip

Simple Subject-Predicate, Exercise 3, page 8.
1. Maria
2. you
3. I
4. you
5. you
6. I
7. chances
8. you
9. you
10. you
11. you
12. you
13. you
14. I
15. you

Simple Subject-Predicate, Exercise 4, page 8.
1. begins
2. Should ask
3. is traveling
4. were
5. Ask
6. watched
7. talks
8. played
9. did clean
10. is broken
11. have been gone
12. decorated
13. Hold
14. is
15. came

Simple Subject-Predicate, Exercise 5, page 9.
1. built
2. stood
3. are
4. ran
5. were tied
6. shone
7. were
8. Do know
9. is
10. has been taken
11. was found
12. ended
13. has
14. complained
15. Clean

Simple Subject-Predicate, Exercise 6, page 9.
1. people/have gone
2. you/Can go
3. We/watched
4. shape/makes
5. group/left
6. you/Help
7. insects/can surprise
8. members/walked
9. clown/wore
10. Children/sat
11. car/was painted
12. person/laughed
13. I/remembered
14. you/did buy
15. John Mills/rode
16. eyes/sparkled
17. He/was running
18. family/will have
19. you/bring
20. Mickey Mouse/had

Compound Subject-Predicate, Exercise 1, page 11.
1. Mom, Dad
2. carrots, beets
3. Dogs, cats, birds, fish
4. Elena, mother
5. Red, yellow, blue
6. He, I
7. Mary, Joan, mother
8. doctor, patient
9. letters, books, newspapers
10. cars, trucks
11. uncle, aunt
12. Jane, Fred, I
13. Violins, violas
14. You, I
15. Pens, pencils, erasers

Compound Subject-Predicate, Exercise 2, page 12.
1. stood, waited
2. dance, sing
3. Clean, cut
4. meets, practices
5. wrote, became
6. walks, rides
7. watched, went
8. coughed, sneezed
9. raked, piled, burned
10. raise, sell
11. return, get
12. drove, bought
13. ran, grabbed, returned
14. wrote, sent
15. ate, read, went
16. went, returned
17. were, had
18. gave, left
19. sat, ate, played
20. grow, have

Compound Subject-Predicate, Exercise 3, page 12.
1. Alice, Maria/laughed, cried
2. /loved, became
3. cat, bird/
4. /ride, drive
5. mother, father/went, bought
6. Trains, cars/
7. /began, lasted
8. Sleet, snow, rain/
9. /poured, drank
10. /call, write
11. Trees, bushes/
12. none
13. Deer, elk, moose
14. Smoke, steam/
15. /walked, barked, lay

Subject-Verb Agreement, Exercise 1, page 13.

1. drives
2. want
3. rises
4. blossom
5. live
6. chase
7. calls
8. wants
9. encourages
10. enjoys
11. runs
12. know
13. fix
14. fixes
15. falls

Subject-Verb Agreement, Exercise 2, page 14.

1. John and Susan
2. am
3. were
4. are
5. are
6. Winter
7. sandwiches and shakes
8. I
9. My parents
10. are

Subject-Verb Agreement, Exercise 3, page 14.

1. are
2. have
3. were
4. make
5. are
6. cause
7. work
8. were
9. close
10. are
11. were
12. cost
13. have
14. are
15. are

Subject-Verb Agreement, Exercise 4, page 15.

Answers will vary.

Sentence Fragments, Exercise 1, page 16.

1. Sentence
2. Fragment
3. Fragment
4. Fragment
5. Fragment
6. Sentence
7. Fragment
8. Fragment
9. Fragment
10. Fragment
11. Sentence
12. Fragment
13. Fragment
14. Fragment
15. Sentence

Sentence Fragments, Exercise 2, page 17.

1. c
2. b
3. a
4. d
5. b
6. d
7. a
8. c
9. d
10. c

Sentence Fragments, Exercise 3, page 17.

Answers will vary.

Simple Sentences, Exercise 1, page 18.

1. d
2. c
3. b
4. a
5. b
6. c
7. c
8. b
9. a
10. a
11. d
12. b
13. c
14. d
15. a

Compound Sentences, Exercise 1, page 20.

1. Simple
2. Compound
3. Simple
4. Compound
5. Compound
6. Simple
7. Simple
8. Compound
9. Simple
10. Compound

Compound Sentences, Exercise 2, page 20.

1. You can drive north, or you can drive where you want
2. The reporter called yesterday, but she didn't come until today.
3. You can take me to the theater, and I will walk home.
4. Can you find out now, or can you ask me later?
5. We went to see the polar bears, but they were resting elsewhere.
6. Some animals are endangered, and they should be protected.
7. You must pay the full price, or you can't buy the clothes.
8. Most people are not disturbed, but some are easily disturbed.
9. She used to play soccer, but now she plays racketball.
10. Call me, and I will come.

Compound Sentences, Exercise 3, page 21.

1. <u>It is raining now</u> (but) <u>it snowed last night</u>.
2. You can bring your boots or shoes.
3. <u>I can finish in no time</u> (or) <u>I can take a long, long time.</u>
4. <u>We went fishing,</u> (and) <u>James caught two fish.</u>
5. <u>She doesn't know why,</u> (but) <u>she can find out</u>.
6. <u>Bring everything,</u> (and) <u>we will know the answer</u>.
7. People ran home or walked quickly by.
8. <u>Cups and saucers are there,</u> (and) <u>forks and knives are here</u>.
9. <u>Our house is closed,</u> (but) <u>your school is not</u>.
10. The computer stopped and never started again.

Compound Sentences, Exercise 4, page 21.
Answers may vary.
1. Our family is planning a vacation. My parents want to go to the ocean, but my brother and I want to go to the mountains.

2. My brother likes to hike, and I like to collect rocks, but our parents aren't interested in hiking or rock collecting.

3. Our parents like to swim and to sun bathe, but we are not the slightest bit interested in swimming or sun bathing.

4. Perhaps our family can go to the beach or to the mountains. Our parents can go their way, and we can go ours.

Run-on Sentences, Exercise 1, page 22.
1. Separate: My brother drove us to the beach. We went swimming.
   Compound: My brother drove us to the beach, and we went swimming.
2. Separate: You think that is the answer. I don't think so.
   Compound: You think that is the answer, but I don't think so.
3. Separate: Regular plates can break. Plastic plates break less often.
   Compound: Regular plates can break, but plastic plates break less often.
4. Separate: Some people finish quickly. They have nothing to do.
   Compound: Some people finish quickly, and they have nothing to do.
5. Separate: I never forget. You never remember.
   Compound: I never forget, and you never remember.

Run-on Sentences, Exercise 2, page 22. Possible answers. There may be variations.
1. You should call, or you should write.
2. I wish you were here, because someone asked for you.
3. I don't like diet soda, but I sometimes drink it at parties.
4. Some people have answers, and some people have questions.
5. I went home, and I called you.

Run-on Sentences, Exercise 3, page 23. There are many variations.
1. He sat at the table. He looked out the window and watched the wind blow. The sky turned dark, and rain fell.
2. They walked down the path and into the woods. Pam climbed a tree. John picked wild flowers.
3. We often buy stale bread and feed the ducks. They swim from all over to get our bread. We enjoy feeding them.
4. (You) Find the telephone book, and (you) look up the number. I will call and order a pizza.
5. The bus stopped, and the door opened. Many people hurried to their jobs. Most people arrived on time.

Sentence Combining, Exercise 1, page 25.
1. No dogs or cats are allowed.
2. Cars, buses, and trucks stopped traffic.
3. You and I checked the water supply.
4. Did Bill or Ann answer the phone?
5. A coat, a hat, and gloves will keep you warm.
6. Martin and Marian travel to Albany each day.
7. Asia and Africa have tall mountains.
8. Neptune, Saturn, and Jupiter are larger than Mercury.
9. John and I were home for the summer.
10. Paint, a brush, and a roller are needed.

Sentence Combining, Exercise 2, page 25.
1. Jane hid behind the bench. I hid behind the bench.
2. Sun weathered the boulders. Wind weathered the boulders. Rain weathered the boulders.
3. Oranges are on sale this week. Apples are on sale this week. Bananas are on sale this week.
4. Those explorers lived years ago. (Those) Inventors lived years ago.
5. Nancy finished the job earlier than expected. Maria finished the job earlier than expected.
6. Cars made deliveries in the early morning. Trucks made deliveries in the early morning.
7. Hard work paid off. Talent paid off. Luck paid off.
8. He will be there at five o'clock. She will be there at five o'clock.
9. The driver arrived late. Her assistant arrived late.
10. Eric will attend the meeting. His brother will attend the meeting.
11. Elena writes newspaper stories. Carol writes newspaper stories.
12. You were in Hawaii last year. I was in Hawaii last year.
13. Fog slows traffic on the freeway. Rain slows traffic on the freeway.
14. Nepal has high mountains. Chile has high mountains.
15. The dog is asleep. The cat is asleep.

Sentence Combining, Exercise 3, page 26.
1. Julia entered the tournament and won.
2. You must go or stay.
3. We helped with painting or went shopping.
4. My father writes, prints, and sells books.
5. She sat by the phone and waited.

Sentence Combining, Exercise 4, page 27.
1. Emily writes her grandmother every week. Emily telephones her grandmother every week.
2. The doctor examined the injured worker. The doctor treated the injured worker. The doctor released the injured worker.
3. I made ornaments. I delivered them.
4. The birds built nests. The birds gathered worms.
5. He completed his work. He left.
6. My sister reads books on Sunday. My sister writes letters on Sunday.
7. The crowd pointed. The crowd cheered.
8. They cut the logs. They stacked the logs. They burned the logs.
9. The sight surprised them. The sight frightened them.
10. (You) Ask her. (You) Hang up.

Sentence Combining, Exercise 5, page 27. Answers can vary.
Emily and Elena walked to the store. They bought a newspaper on the way and mailed letters.
They returned home and put the groceries away. Cans and bottles were put in the cupboard.
Meat and vegetables were put in the refrigerator.

Emily cut bread and made sandwiches. Elena poured milk and set the table. They ate lunch
and went outside.

Final Assessment Test, page 28.

A. Subject-Predicate. Draw a vertical line between the complete subject and the complete predicate. Underline the simple subject once. Underline the simple predicate twice.

    1. (you) | Can <u>call</u> my parents?

    2. <u>Elena</u>, <u>Marie</u>, and <u>Philip</u> | <u>attended</u> the concert.

    3. The loud <u>noise</u> | <u>startled</u> or <u>frightened</u> everyone.

    4. <u>She</u> | <u>cut</u>, <u>stacked</u>, and <u>covered</u> the wood.

    5. The two young <u>children</u> | <u>watched</u>.

    6. (You) | <u>Calm</u> down!

    7. <u>Alice</u> and <u>John</u> | <u>laughed</u> and <u>cried</u>.

B. Subject-Verb Agreement. Choose the correct word in parentheses then fill in the blank.

    1. You and he (is, **are**) to meet here later.

    2. A hot dog and chips (**cost**, costs) two dollars.

    3. They (was, **were**) thirsty.

    4. _____ have ordered their dinner.

    5. _____ are waiting for us.   **Answers will vary.**

    6. _____ follows me home everyday.

C. Sentence Structures. Identify each sentence as one of the following: a simple sentence, a compound sentence, a sentence fragment, or a run-on sentence.

    1. The bus stopped and everybody got off and they crossed the street. **Run-on**

    2. (You) Be sure to call me. **Simple**

    3. Hundreds of people. **Fragment**

    4. My brother hid, and I counted to twenty. **Compound**

    5. My brother and I counted and hid. **Simple**

D. Sentence Combining. Combine the three sentences in Part 1 to make a simple sentence. Combine the two sentences in Part 2 to make a compound sentence.

    1. The chicken is cooked. The corn is cooked. The beans are cooked.

    2. You bought socks. I bought socks.

    1. The chicken, corn, and beans are cooked.

    2. You bought socks, and I bought socks.